CREATIVE EDUCATION

CHICAGO BEARS

JOHN NICHOLS

Published by Creative Education
123 South Broad Street, Mankato, Minnesota 56001
Creative Education is an imprint of The Creative Company

Designed by Rita Marshall

Photos by: Allsport USA, AP/Wide World Photos, Bettmann/CORBIS,
SportsChrome

Library of Congress Cataloging-in-Publication Data

Nichols, John, 1966–
Chicago Bears / by John Nichols.
p. cm. — (NFL today)
Summary: Traces the history of the team from its beginnings through 1999.
ISBN 1-58341-039-2

1. Chicago Bears (Football team)—History—Juvenile literature.
[1. Chicago Bears (Football team). 2. Football—History.] I. Title.
II. Series: NFL today (Mankato, Minn.)

GV956.C5N53   2000
796.332'64'0977311—dc21   99-015743

First edition

9 8 7 6 5 4 3 2 1

October 16, 1921, was a fairly typical Sunday in Chicago, Illinois. It was a beautiful autumn afternoon in the city on Lake Michigan's southern shore. Most of Chicago's citizens were enjoying a break from what was then a six-day work week. One young man, however, was too busy and nervous to relax.

George Halas, a 26-year-old athlete and entrepreneur, planned to introduce his professional football team, the Chicago Bears, to the people of the Windy City that afternoon. The contest was to be played at Cubs Park (the future Wrigley Field), and the cost of a ticket was one dollar.

"Papa Bear" George Halas (far right).

Halas and his partner, Dutch Sternaman, had each paid $100 to the Staley Starch Company in nearby Decatur to purchase its semi-pro team, the Decatur Staleys. They then renamed the team the Bears and moved it to Chicago. The two men hoped to sell enough tickets to at least cover expenses and earn back their investment. Nearly 8,000 spectators came out on that first Sunday afternoon to cheer for the team in midnight blue and orange. It was a rousing start.

Those fans could not have guessed that the Chicago Bears would, over the next eight decades, win more than 600 games, capture nine National Football League championships—including one Super Bowl—and secure berths in the Pro Football Hall of Fame for a record 24 team members, including Halas himself.

PAPA BEAR

Throughout the club's history, the Chicago Bears have been more than a team. They have been a family, held together for their first 60 years by "Papa Bear" George Halas, who held sole ownership of the team.

In the team's early days, Halas also sold tickets, taped ankles, shoveled snow, coached, and occasionally played defense. In one game against the Oorang Indians, who were led by running back Jim Thorpe, Halas put himself in at defensive end, recovered a Thorpe fumble, and raced 98 yards for a Chicago touchdown. Halas served as the Bears' coach for four separate stints between 1921 and 1967. He won NFL championships at age 26 and at age 68, and of the 40 teams he coached, only six finished with losing records.

Deep-threat receiver Marcus Robinson.

1 9 2 5

Red Grange signed a contract with the Bears for the astronomical sum of $100,000.

Halas was a man of many firsts. He was the first NFL coach to schedule daily practices, the first to study game films, the first to scout small colleges for talent, and the first to introduce a team song. But above all, Halas was the first man to dream that football could become a first-class, big-league sport. Halas's dreams for professional football in Chicago might not have come true, though, if he had not recruited two exceptional running backs—Harold "Red" Grange and Bronko Nagurski.

Grange, known as "the Galloping Ghost," signed with the Bears on November 22, 1925, after a legendary career at the University of Illinois. In those days, college football was big news in America, while pro football seldom made the headlines. Grange would change all that. The Bears began an amazing cross-country tour on Thanksgiving Day in 1925, playing 19 games in 66 days, including eight in a 12-day period. "Those 66 days made professional football," a *Sports Illustrated* writer later noted. In one game at New York's Polo Grounds, a record 73,000 people turned out to see Grange and his teammates defeat the Giants 19–7, starting a major rivalry between the two clubs.

Grange's importance to the Bears extended well past 1925. He anchored the club throughout its early years, caught the winning pass in the 1932 NFL championship game, and made a game-saving tackle at the end of the 1933 title game.

During the 1930 season, Grange was joined in the Bears' backfield by a bruising runner named Bronislau Nagurski. Better known as "Bronko," this unstoppable force played for the Bears until 1937, then came out of retirement for a final season in 1943 at Halas's request. Nagurski's bone-jarring runs were his trademark. In one game, he blasted through two tacklers, raced across the end zone, and ran full speed into a brick retaining wall. Merely shaking his head, on which he wore only a flimsy leather helmet, Nagurski trotted back to the bench and remarked, "That last guy really gave me a good lick."

Not many things could stop Chicago in the early 1930s. In 1932, Grange and Nagurski combined for one of the greatest plays in Bears history. In the championship game against the Portsmouth Spartans, the game was scoreless in the fourth quarter. The Bears took the ball and began driving, feeding Nagurski the ball on almost every play. On fourth-and-goal from the two-yard line, Bronko took the ball once again. As a wall of Portsmouth tacklers rose up in front of him, he stopped short, leaped up, and tossed a short pass to Grange for the winning touchdown.

The two Chicago stars teamed up to lead the Bears to a second consecutive championship in 1933 and to the title game in 1934. Though Father Time eventually caught up with them toward the end of the decade, the Galloping Ghost and Bronko were both ultimately enshrined in the Hall of Fame.

1 9 3 6

Fearsome runner Bronko Nagurski hammered through defenses for 529 rushing yards.

LUCKY WITH LUCKMAN

With Chicago's backfield legends at the end of their careers, Halas needed someone to lead the Bears back to the top. In 1939, Papa Bear drafted a tailback from Columbia University named Sid Luckman and transformed him

10 *Neal Anderson scared defenses with his speed and elusive moves.*

Hall of Fame linebacker Mike Singletary.

1 9 4 3

Sid Luckman became the first pro quarterback to pass for more than 400 yards in a single game.

from a runner to a passer. With Luckman at quarterback, a new Bears dynasty began.

From 1940 to 1943, Luckman led the Bears to an incredible 37–5–1 record, four Western Division titles, and three NFL championships. Luckman and other Bears stars such as center Clyde "Bulldog" Turner, halfback George McAfee, and tackle Joe Stydahar (all eventual Hall-of-Famers) played some outstanding football games during those four seasons, but no contest came as close to perfection as the 1940 NFL championship game against the Washington Redskins—the first game ever broadcast to a national radio audience.

Just three weeks earlier, Washington had beaten the Bears 7–3 on a controversial call. When the Bears complained, Redskins owner George Marshall told the press that the Bears were "quitters and a bunch of crybabies."

Halas was furious. He took the press clippings and plastered them on the locker room walls. Then he gave his team an inspiring pep talk. He ended by saying, "Gentlemen, this is what the Redskins think of you. I think you're a great football team—the greatest ever assembled. Go out onto the field and prove it."

Spurred on by pride and anger, the Bears destroyed Washington 73–0 in the most lopsided pro football game of all time. It got so bad that, at one point, the referees approached George Halas and asked if he would stop kicking extra points. So many balls had been booted into the stands that the Redskins were down to their last football.

"Some observers said the Bears were a perfect football team that day," said Halas. "I can't agree. Looking over the movies, I can see where we should have scored another touchdown."

Sid Luckman's Chicago dynasty was slowed down by World War II, as many of the team's top players left to join the armed forces. The club resumed its winning ways with an NFL championship in 1946 and some fine play throughout the rest of the decade. Luckman's retirement after the 1951 season marked the end of the second golden era in Bears history.

The Bears' fortunes took a dive during the rest of the 1950s. Still, the teams of those years featured some exceptional talent. Running backs Rick Casares and Willie Galimore excited fans with their speed and power; quarterbacks Ed Brown and Bill Wade were solid leaders; Johnny Morris and Harlon Hill were outstanding receivers; and no one was tougher than middle linebacker Bill George. But it wasn't enough.

Fullback Rick Casares led the NFL in rushing with 1,126 yards and 12 touchdowns.

The Bears rolled to the 1940 NFL title.

George Halas, who had given up head coaching duties in the mid-1950s, decided that the team needed him back at the controls in 1958. Sure enough, the Bears began edging their way back up the NFL standings. By 1963, Halas and his right-hand man, defensive coordinator George Allen, guided the Bears back to the NFL championship game against their archrivals, the New York Giants. The Giants, led by quarterback Y.A. Tittle and running back Frank Gifford, were heavy favorites. But Allen's defenders shut down the powerful New York offense, intercepting five Tittle passes in a 14–10 Bears upset victory.

1 9 6 0

Fierce linebacker Bill George made the sixth of eight straight Pro Bowl appearances.

THREE OF THE BEST

The Bears didn't stay on top for long, but the team did soon acquire two special stars—Dick Butkus and Gale Sayers—who would excite Windy City fans for years. Halas selected both players in the 1965 college draft, and they quickly became gridiron legends.

Dick Butkus was a dominant defensive force, but there was nothing pretty about the way he played. He was notorious for his hard hitting and nasty disposition. "Butkus was the epitome of the middle linebacker," said Mike Ditka, a teammate for several years. "He played the game from the tip of his head to the bottom of his soles."

While Butkus represented brute strength on the field, Gale Sayers epitomized gracefulness. He was an outstanding rusher, receiver, and kick returner—perhaps the best all-around offensive star in NFL history. During one game against the San Francisco 49ers in his rookie season, Sayers

Legendary runner Walter Payton.

Feared middle linebacker Dick Butkus.

scored a remarkable six touchdowns—one on a pass, two on end sweeps, two on power dives up the middle, and the last on an 85-yard zigzagging punt return. "He's no different from any other runner when he's coming at you," noted a 49ers defender, "but when he gets there, he's gone."

Bad knees forced Sayers into early retirement in 1971. Six years later, at the age of 34, he became the youngest member ever elected to the Hall of Fame. Butkus, who retired after the 1973 season, joined Sayers in the Hall of Fame in 1979.

In the decade between 1966 and 1975, the Bears had only one winning season. But the last year of that losing streak also marked the arrival of Chicago's next legendary backfield star: Walter Payton.

Walter Payton was born and raised in Columbia, Mississippi. In high school, Payton played drums in the band and joined the gymnastics team. When he finally decided to go out for football, however, it was obvious that Payton was a natural. He ran for a 61-yard touchdown in his first high school game. After an outstanding college career at Jackson State in Mississippi, Payton continued his dominant ways as a professional player.

"Sweetness," as Payton was nicknamed, was tough on opposing defenders. In keeping with Bears tradition, Payton loved hard-nosed play. In his 10th season in Chicago, he was nearing Jim Brown's NFL career rushing record of 12,312 yards. A reporter asked Payton how he would like to break the mark. Payton replied, "I want to go up the middle, hit one guy, bounce off, hit another, jump over someone, and fight for the extra yard." Payton not only surpassed

1 9 6 5

Graceful halfback Gale Sayers scored an NFL-record 22 touchdowns in his rookie season.

The Bears have always been known for their rugged play (18-19).

Brown's record, he shattered it, ending his career in 1987 with 16,726 yards rushing.

The quiet Payton always gave credit to his linemen and presented each of them with an engraved gold watch after he broke Brown's mark in 1984. But what Payton and his teammates really wanted were Super Bowl rings.

Tackle Wally Chambers led the "Monsters of the Midway" with 14 quarterback sacks.

"IRON MIKE" DITKA

George Halas also longed for another championship ring. Though he felt he was too old to coach the Bears to victory again, he knew the right man for the job—Mike Ditka, a former Bears tight end.

Ditka had played on the last Chicago championship team in 1963. During six seasons in Chicago, Ditka caught 316 passes for more than 4,500 yards to rank among the all-time team leaders. He also threw some devastating blocks to protect his quarterback or to open holes for Bears runners. Known as "Iron Mike," he was emotional and sometimes hotheaded, but he knew how to win. Most importantly, he bled navy blue, orange, and white. "I was always a Bear," admitted Ditka. "Even when I was playing and coaching in Dallas, I was a Chicago Bear."

Ditka had a wealth of talent awaiting him when he came back to Chicago before the 1982 season. The defense was anchored by standout end Dan Hampton, linebacker Mike Singletary, and safety Gary Fencik. On offense were Payton and a rookie quarterback from Brigham Young University named Jim McMahon. Ditka's job was to take these thoroughbreds to the race and win.

Unfortunately, George Halas would not be there in the winner's circle. Papa Bear died of a heart attack on October 31, 1983. The Bears' owner for 62 years was also one of the greatest coaches in NFL history—with a career record of 326–151–31—and the Bears' biggest fan.

Wearing black bands with the initials "GSH" on their sleeves to honor Halas's memory, Ditka's Bears clawed their way to 8–8 in 1983, then captured the NFC Central Division title in 1984 with a 10–6 record. Walter Payton contributed 1,684 rushing yards that year to key the offense, but it was Chicago's defense that led the way. Chicago overcame the powerful Washington Redskins for a 23–19 first-round play-off win but was unable to halt the San Francisco 49ers in the NFC title game. The 49ers went on to capture the Super

Coach Mike Ditka guided the Bears to the first of five consecutive Central Division titles.

All-Pro defensive tackle Dan Hampton.

End Richard Dent led a hard-hitting Bears defense in the 1980s.

Bowl in 1984, but Bears players and fans were certain that their time on top would come soon.

Soon turned out to be the next year. The Bears won their first 12 games in 1985 en route to a stellar 15–1 record. Once again, defense was the key. Five Chicago defenders were named All-Pro that year, with tackle Richard Dent leading the league in sacks and linebacker Mike Singletary being named the Defensive Player of the Year. Also featured was a 320-pound rookie named William Perry, whose nickname, "the Refrigerator," referred either to his size or to his favorite place in the house. Perry, a defensive tackle, even played fullback on occasion when the Bears wanted a gigantic blocker or runner in the game. On offense, Payton gained 1,551 yards, and McMahon threw for 2,392 more.

In the playoffs, the Bears defenders shut down the New York Giants 21–0 to propel the team to the NFC championship game against the Los Angeles Rams. The fearsome Bears defense again shut the door on the Rams, while McMahon led the Chicago offense to a 24–0 win and the team's first Super Bowl berth.

In Super Bowl XX, Chicago's shutout streak ended when the New England Patriots scored on a first-period field goal to go up 3–0, but that lead was short-lived. Chicago scored the next 44 points on their way to a 46–10 rout. Mike Ditka and the Bears were the toast of the town once again.

The Bears continued to dominate the NFC's Central Division from 1986 through 1988, winning their third, fourth, and fifth consecutive division titles and earning playoff berths each year. During that five-year span, the Bears won a total of 62 games—the most ever by any NFL team. How-

1 9 8 6

Jim McMahon passed for 250 yards as the Bears won the Super Bowl.

Veteran center Jay Hildenburg was the lone representative of the Bears offense in the Pro Bowl.

ever, Chicago fell to the Redskins in the postseason in both 1986 and 1987 and to the 49ers in the 1988 NFC championship game.

The late 1980s saw the emergence of several new Bears stars as many of the old standouts retired or were traded. Payton stepped down in 1987 and was ultimately elected to the Hall of Fame in 1993. His replacement at running back, Neal Anderson, filled the gap by rushing for 1,000 yards three years in a row. Mike Tomczak and Jim Harbaugh shared quarterbacking duties in place of Jim McMahon, and new defensive standouts included safety Dave Duerson and tackles Trace Armstrong and Steve McMichael.

After a disappointing 6–10 campaign in 1989, the Bears bounced back with 11–5 seasons in both 1990 and 1991. But

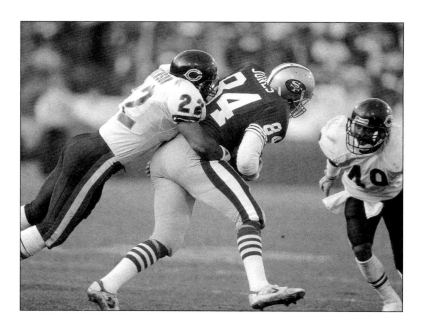

Star safety Dave Duerson (left).

after a 5–11 campaign in 1992, Bears management decided that Ditka's blend of emotion and intimidation was no longer what the club needed. Iron Mike left the Bears after piling up 112 victories during his 11 seasons at the helm—a victory total second only to that of Papa Bear Halas.

WANNSTEDT'S BATTLING BEARS

First-year coach Dave Wannstedt led Chicago to a 7–9 record.

Before the 1993 season, the Bears selected Dave Wannstedt as the man who would replace the beloved Mike Ditka on the Soldier Field sidelines. Wannstedt came to the Bears after a brilliant run as defensive coordinator for the Dallas Cowboys. During his four years in Dallas, he had put together a swarming defense that spurred the Cowboys to a Super Bowl victory in 1992.

Wannstedt was hired to rebuild an aging Bears team, and he wasted little time. Stalwarts such as Pro-Bowlers Richard Dent and Neal Anderson departed and were replaced by younger players such as defensive end Alonzo Spellman and halfback Rashaan Salaam.

Unfortunately for Coach Wannstedt, many of the new players he counted on would not be up to the task. Salaam was a good example of the Bears' misfortunes in the mid-1990s. The Colorado University product had been a college superstar, winning the Heisman Trophy as the nation's finest player in 1994. As Chicago's top draft pick in 1995, he was expected to blossom into the next great Bears halfback.

At first, the swift and powerful Salaam was impressive, gaining 1,074 yards in his rookie year on his way to what seemed sure stardom. Over the next two years, however,

A hard-nosed runner in the Bears tradition, Curtis Enis (pages 26-27).

Salaam was beset by numerous nagging injuries and a tendency to fumble. By 1997, the young rusher's career in Chicago was over. The end came with a badly broken leg.

With their young players struggling and their older players fading, Wannstedt's Bears slipped from contender status, posting 4–12 seasons in 1997 and 1998. Over his six seasons in Chicago, Wannstedt's Bears were consistently short on talent but long on heart and feistiness. "Dave's teams don't have a lot of star-quality guys on the roster," noted Minnesota Vikings coach Dennis Green, "but he gets them to play hard for 60 minutes."

Unfortunately for Wannstedt, the bad luck that followed the Bears would cost him his job after the 1998 season. Chicago would look to rebuild once again.

1 9 9 7

Jim Flanigan led Chicago's defensive line with 81 tackles and six sacks.

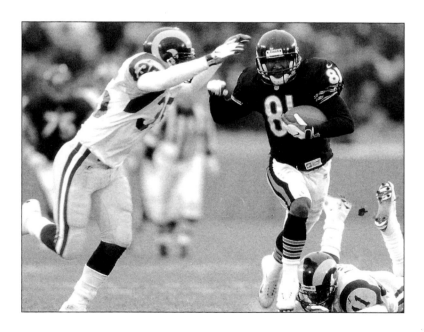

Multitalented receiver Bobby Engram.

A New Hope with Jauron

After Wannstedt was fired, Chicago hired the coach it felt would bring greatness back to the historic franchise. Dick Jauron accepted the Bears' head coaching position after spending four years as the Jacksonville Jaguars' defensive coordinator. "Dick has a very disciplined approach," said Jacksonville head coach Tom Coughlin. "He knows what it's like to build with young players. The Bears have made a great choice."

Jauron would build with youth, but the Bears also had several talented veterans to rely on. Acrobatic wide receiver Curtis Conway gave the team a big-play threat, and talented running back Curtis Enis was the sort of hard-nosed ball-carrier that Chicago fans love. On the other side of the ball, defensive tackle Jim Flanigan and cornerback Walt Harris led a feisty Bears defense.

Among the youngsters, the Bears looked for quarterback Cade McNown to be a key offensive catalyst. The 1999 first-round draft pick from UCLA came to Chicago with a reputation for turning broken plays into big gains. "Cade never gives up on a play," said Coach Jauron. "He'll scramble and make something out of nothing. He's one tough kid."

Despite the addition of McNown, most football experts expected little from the Bears in 1999. As the season wore on, however, the Bears proved they were anything but a door-mat. Rising stars such as receivers Marcus Robinson and Bobby Engram provided surprising offensive punch, while end Bryan Robinson and veteran linebacker Barry Minter helped anchor a solid defense.

1 9 9 9

Marcus Robinson emerged as a star, catching 84 passes for 1,400 yards.

Scrappy quarterback Cade McNown.

The leader of the Bears defense, tackle Jim Flanigan.   31

Defensive back Tony Parrish was expected to add toughness to the Bears defense.

Though given limited playing time, McNown proved to be a great draft pick. Playing his first game as a starter late in the season, the rookie put on a dazzling show, throwing for 301 yards and four touchdowns to lead the Bears to a 28–10 victory over Detroit.

The Bears also drew inspiration from the death of one of the team's all-time greats. Walter Payton, stricken with a rare liver disease, died on November 1 at the age of 45. The following Sunday, the Bears defeated the Packers 14–13. "That one was for Sweetness," said offensive tackle James Williams. "I know he would be proud."

Losses in the final two games of the season kept the Bears out of the playoffs with a 6–10 mark, but Chicago went into the off-season as one of the NFL's up-and-coming teams. "I'm certain the guys are disappointed," Coach Jauron said. "But they have to remember where we started, and more importantly, where we are going."

The off-season addition of powerful rookie linebacker Brian Urlacher should continue to boost Chicago in the NFC Central. Tough guys have always found a place in the hearts of Chicago fans. Now, with a host of new stars ready to bare their teeth, these Bears are looking to become "Monsters of the Midway" once again.